P9-CDS-785

My First Biography

Christopher Columbus

by Marion Dane Bauer
Illustrated by Liz Goulet Dubois

SCHOLASTIC INC.
New York   Toronto   London   Auckland
Sydney   Mexico City   New Delhi   Hong Kong

Genoa

ITALY

ISBN 978-0-545-14232-8

Text copyright © 2009 by Marion Dane Bauer
Illustrations copyright © 2009 by Liz Goulet Dubois

12 11 10 9 8 7 6 5 4 3 2 1   10 11 12 13 14 15/0
Printed in the U.S.A.   40
This edition first printing, August 2010

Book design by Jennifer Rinaldi Windau

Christopher Columbus was a dreamer when he was a boy.

He dreamed of sailing the Ocean Sea.

When he grew into a man,
Christopher Columbus was still a dreamer.

He dreamed of reaching the Indies
by sailing around the world.

Columbus needed sailors and ships
to make his dream come true.

He asked the king of Portugal for help.

The king said, "No."

He asked the king and queen of Spain for help.

The king and queen said, "No."

He asked again.
Again they said, "No."

And again they said, "No."

But Columbus kept asking.

After many years the king and queen finally said, "Yes."

Columbus sailed into the unknown
with ninety sailors and three ships.

The ships were the *Niña*, the *Pinta*, and the *Santa María*.

They sailed the ocean for over nine weeks.

"We will never see land again!" the sailors wept.

But only a few days later,
one of the sailors spotted something.

"*Tierra! Tierra!*" he cried. "Land! Land!"

Columbus knelt on the ground and
gave thanks for their safe arrival.

He thought he had arrived in the East Indies.

He called the gentle people
who came to greet him "Indians."

Columbus never knew that his dream had brought him to a new land—the Americas!

Columbus dreamed the dream.
He showed the way.
Many others followed.